D.I.B.B.L.E.

D.I.B.B.L.E.

Dr. Darlene Adamson-Henderson

XULON PRESS

Xulon Press
2301 Lucien Way #415
Maitland, FL 32751
407.339.4217
www.xulonpress.com

Printed in the United States of America.

Paperback ISBN-13: 978-1-6305-0816-6

eBook ISBN-13: 978-1-6305-0817-3

Dedication Tribute

I dedicate "DIBBLE" to my mother: Dollie L. Adamson, a phenomenal woman and the greatest teacher of excellence and example sent from heaven to earth.

Your passion to teach still radiates in the earth through the many lives you touched.

You will forever be remembered and celebrated.

Your Darling Daughter Darlene

Endorsements

DO IT BLISSFULLY BEFORE LEAVING EARTH: Is a must read for everyone. Darlene has always had a gift for words: poetry, speaking, preaching, the list goes on. I pondered on this word and decided to look it up. The word dibble is a tool used in boring. Boring is to force an opening or make a passage. I revealed to Darlene that this book is a passage to a great gift from God. His blessing of salvation and life with Him. He wants us to choose to be happy, blissfully happy. God wants to bless us which means to make happy. This book is a gift which will lead you to understand the love of God and how he truly wants us to be happy and the only way is through Jesus our Savior. THIS IS A MUST READ!!

Prophetess Miriam Adamson Tangle
Retired Specialized Services Administraor For
Milwaukee Public Schools, WI

Unquestionably, Dr. Henderson has received God's Prophetic Mandate via DIBBLE, to serve as a forerunner, paving The Way for The Return of our Christ. Such as John the Baptist, in the spirit and power of Elijah, to turn the hearts of the fathers to the children and the disobedient to the wisdom of the just; to make ready a people prepared for The LORD.
Congratulations: MISSION ACCOMPLISHED!

Apostle Rudy Gray
The Love Church

Dr. Darlene Adamson Henderson has laid out a plan for a more prosperous and abundant life in this Roadmap leading to Eternal Life with our Father. It is a plan that is facilitated by the Love of God. Her life itself has been a model testament for others to know that joy comes as a result of servitude to our Lord and Savior, Jesus Christ. I highly recommend every believer as well as non-believers would read this Awe-inspiring book. The title, "DIBBLE" itself pulls you in!

If we truly believe the word of God, then by it we know that Jesus is coming back again soon! We are witnesses to the signs of our time according to the bible.

Ernestine May
Author of, "*Life is a Story*",
An autobiography of her life and how every
motivating accomplishment is a credit to God.

Dr. Darlene Henderson has a unique gift in that she is able to take Christ our LORD's Biblical Truths and teach them in a way that is relevant and life changing!

Dr. Henderson's Book–"Do It Blissfully Before Leaving Earth" is a book that is truly needed in these times in which we now live. It points to the sovereignty of the LORD God over the issues that man encounters in life and offers Godly wisdom that promotes spiritual growth and enables us to triumph victoriously over life's adversities and challenges!

Congratulations on choosing this "must read" book!

Elder Gwendolyn D. Robinson
Face 2 Face Worship Center,
Evangelism Outreach Director,
Clinton, MD

"She's my Darling Darlene!" These words were spoken to me by the Spirit of God while working with Dr. Darlene Adamson Henderson during the 80's at Kennedy King Middle School in Gary, Indiana. We would often have lunch and prayer time together. I got to know and love her as my dear sister in the Lord and a passionate lover of God and His Word. I refer to her as, My Darling Darlene. The name Darlene means Tenderly Loved and people with this name have a deep desire to inspire others in a higher cause, and to share their own strongly held views on spiritual matters.

DIBBLE is a perfect expression of this belief and it comes straight from my Darling Darlene's heart and the profound, personal relationship that she has with our Lord and Savior Jesus Christ.

It doesn't matter if you are a seasoned saint on this spiritual journey or just beginning, reading DIBBLE will enhance your belief in God's Word and provide you with Seven Key Choice Principles for living a blissful life in Christ while here in Earth.

Jesus is coming back soon!

Gloria Sharpe Smith
God's Daughter
Sugar Land, Texas

DIBBLE is certainly a book that needs to be on any bookshelf. It restarts the mind to think about, if you're really living your life right and where are you going(death) based on the choices you made when you leave earth. This book takes you to a different level of focusing on the reality of your outcome based on those choices.

Carol J King
Founding Board Member Of HIAT School

WOW!! Is all I can say after reading this guide book.

If you are looking for a straightforward road map; DIBLLE is it!

Concise and precise; this book gives you a brief but descriptive pathway for studying how to live happy in God's word.

Dr. Henderson pulls no punches and uses scripture to back it up. If you are serious about learning, living, studying God's way this word goes into a deeper level of spiritual awareness. Start here and taste the fruits and nuggets she delivers. You won't be disappointed.

Dr. Ruthie Jimerson
Retired Proprietor of Amazing Dental After Hours
Former Advisory Board member for HIAT School

"DIBBLE–Do It Blissfully Before Leaving Earth" holds keys to serving God with purity and passion while you are still in the earth realm and preparing for His return by living His word now.

This book allows us to demonstrate our love for Father God through obedience to His Word and allowing people to experience His love through us.

Blessings!

Patricia Simes
Business & Entrepreneurship Coach
Innovative Business Solutions, LLC

Dr. Darlene Adamson Henderson,

"You have captured the fact that We shall not cease from exploring the end and at the end of our exportation, we will be able to arrive where we started and know the awesome place for the first time. There is nothing so exciting as knowing that the past is forgotten and new options are ahead."

People hunger to be free,

V.A.Hill
No More Burnt Toast

Dibble is certainly a book for everyone's list of must reads. Learning how to make choices that are life changing with such a positive outcome is vital to our existence. Darlene does an excellent job clarifying the choices that bring us to the ultimate dream. Her anointed words if heeded are transformative.

Blessings!

Sharon Wachowiak
Author & President of Lionheart Ministries

Acknowledgments

First and utmost, I'd like to thank my Lord and Savior Jesus the Christ, the greatest love of my life, for giving me the strength and insight to write *DIBBLE*, my little book of instruction for eternal life. God, I love you so much. There's no love that can compare to your love. You are so amazing! Thank you for allowing me to be your vessel of faith to open your school HIAT.

Second, I'd like to thank my husband, Booker T. Henderson II, the second love of my life and the wind beneath my wings for being a great support in all of my endeavors I strive for, which have been many. You will never know how much I appreciate and love you. You have been the reason why I'm so motivated for my destiny.

The next greatest loves of my life are my children, DarNieshia and her husband Terrance, the dynamic duo who are my protectors and my radical supporters.

Binika is my own personal angel, prolific advisor, and realtor who has been my personal assistant in all of my endeavors. Your encouraging words from Joel Osteen and your personal angel are so greatly appreciated with your most prophetic words throughout my journeys.

Jamarr, my one and only son is my protector, and "attorney in the making" who has always inspired me to stay strong and pursue the great things God has in store for me especially through my tough journeys.

Jasmine, my sweet angel and my youngest daughter whom God foretold would be born, is so creative and sweet, gifted in graphic design and assistance in creating my cover for *DIBBLE*. Whatever I dream, Jasmine creates it so vividly so I can see everything so blissfully.

My granddaughter Dariyan is my evangelist, encourager, athelete, and is gifted in music and so adventurous.

My twin grandsons, Tyse and Tyres are my sweet inspirations who are also prophets, and my inspiration for the creation of HIAT School. Tyse, whom I call "Dr. Tyse", said, "Nana, you are our own doctor and heal us when we are sick." He is an orator and is gifted in the arts. Tyres is gifted in technology. They are gifted athletes. In *DIBBLE,* there are definite healing remedies and answers.

I continuously celebrate my mother, Dollie L. Adamson, the greatest teacher in Earth and now in heaven. Even though she's in heaven, I can still internally hear her voice of inspiration, instruction, and correction. Early in life, she said, "Darlene, you should consider getting your PhD." I thought it was crazy and a farfetched suggestion at that time, but as you will know, God opened the avenue and enabled me to pursue my doctorate and my mom's prophetic words came true. I'm so thankful for that journey that is still blossoming. I thank my father, Vernon L. Adamson Sr. who was an artist and my brother Vernon L. Adamson Jr., who was a technician.

I thank Booker and Thelma Henderson, my dad and mother-in-love, who have been such a great support in all of my endeavors. Dad was such an instructor in leadership being a leader himself. Mom was a community activist and a remarkable historian with a spirit of excellence.

I celebrate and thank my only younger sister, Miriam R. Tangle, the administrator and prophetess who has been more like my older sister. She always gives me wisdom and puts the icing on the cake in all of my endeavors, and knows exactly how to produce excellence in instruction, education, and in religion. She was instrumental in assisting me in pursuing my higher education. *DIBBLE* has a touch of her in it.

Thanks to my paternal Adamson family and maternal Frazier family. Also extended Morris family: Sisters Joyce & Laurel. I would like to thank two special friends Sharla Johnson and Patricia Bell who became like sisters and Denise Walton who became like a special daughter. Without all of my family and associates, *DIBBLE* and HIAT School wouldn't have landed on planet Earth.

I'm so grateful for my spiritual parents Apostle James and Prophetess Sharon Randolph, overseers of Advancing Christ Kingdom Global Ministries (ACKGM), who greatly assisted in the manifestation of *DIBBLE*. Apostle, you stated I would write books of instruction, and when I began to write *DIBBLE*, I realized it was a book of instruction inspired by God. Prophetess Sharon, you stated I could finish my book if I stayed off the phone. As I purposed to complete *DIBBLE*, I met God at five-thirty each morning. He continued to whisper and became louder: "Finish the book!" I finished the first draft March 31, 2019. I began writing *DIBBLE* in 2017. It was at AvCKGM that prayer and intercession birthed and opened "HIAT", Heritage Institute of Arts and Technology School on September 6, 2016.

Much gratitude is given to Dr. Mildred C. Harris, my mother of Zion, pioneer, prolific, prophetic instructor, prophetess, and overseer of God First Ministries, Signatures of Prolific Women, Gary Educators for Christ, and the CHA Commissioner of Chicago, IL. You spoke HIAT School into existence over twenty years before it manifested. You also said I would write books and *DIBBLE* is my first book of instruction.

Thanks to 'The Love Church Family", Apostle Rudy Gray, overseer whose prophesies are still manifesting, Denise, Atty. Joann, Dr. Vernetha, Theresa, Lillian, Marcy, Angel, Jan, & Alice who all loved and supported me and still do! Much gratitude is given to Ministers Larry & Marla Haak of New Hope Ministries for your continual counsel, support, and prayers for me.

Mrs. Jean Preston, I thank you for being a mother, instructor, and motivator with such words of wisdom that have impacted my life beyond measure, especially in the writing of *DIBBLE* and the opening of Heritage Institute of Arts and Technology (HIAT). Thanks to Mr. Maurice Preston Sr. who blessed me with business savvy life treasures in the business arena.

Thank you Interfaith Prayer Power Pool (IPPP) leaders Mrs. Preston & Rev. Vera & Members.

Gratitude is given to Friday Morning Prayer with Chris & sisters for your prayers, support and love.

I'm so thankful to Interfaith Clergy Council (ICC) for your prayers and support under the leadership of Bishop Dale Cudjoe & Dr. David Neville.

Thank you Dr. & Mrs. Dennis Woods of "Couples Mentoring Youth & Family Services for your prayers and support over the years.

Thank you Gwendolyn Robinson, my cousin and "big sister", who God uses to continuously encourage me in all of my endeavors, especially when I was filled with the Holy Ghost. Before HIAT opened, she would say, "HIAT is already open in heaven."

Special thanks to Carol King, my best friend since kindergarten, who has always been so supportive, kind, and my loving friend forever.

Thanks to Katrina Moten and Artesta Lewis my prophetesses and intercessors who blessed me with prophetic instructions before I knew about prophesies.

Much gratitude to Dr. Carlton Davis & Dr. Nellie Williams from GMOR Theological Institute of America.

Thanks to Ernestine (my first business partner), Gloria S., Rita, Gloria T., Evelyn, Detrice & Doretha whose lives were exemplary of Godly education, excellence and experience which touched my life tremendously while teaching, and being a part of Gary Educators for Christ & TABS (Tuesday Afterschool Bible Study).

Thanks, Big Sis. Debrah, Dr. Ruthie, Vincent, Leona, Dr. Mary, Denise W, Debra W., Mae, Charlotte, Darlene P. who always supported me in in all of my endevors.

Thanks to Erricka Coleman, Dr. Jill Karn & Linda Romo who God sent to help with HIAT, who lovelingly worked tirelessly and took me to the next level in excellence and professionalism, and worked with me to the dawn of many days to complete the work for HIAT School to manifest during my journey of life.

Thank You Everyone!

Foreword

How wonderful and exciting it is for me to have been given the opportunity, to express my sentiments to a beautiful and talented daughter in Christ. Darlene, has written this book truly under the inspiration of the Holy Spirit. Praise God!

The readers of this book will be motivated and challenged to seek God with a hunger and thirst for the deeper things of God.

Upon reading page after page of "DIBBLE" may a greater portion of God's wisdom and knowledge be yours for the asking- as this is what I have received.

Praise Ye The Lord!

With Love in Christ,
A Mother In Zion
Dr. Mildred C. Harris

Foreword

I am humbled and honored to write the foreword of this extremely powerful and necessary book written by **Dr. Darlene Adamson Henderson**. Let me first of all acknowledge this wonderful, honorable and outstanding person that is now an author. Dr. Henderson is really somebody very special to my wife and I who have had the pleasure of her humble service. She is very wise, gifted, classy, family focused, educated, honorable, passionate, dedicated and extremely humble. All that we have known about her over the years has been confirmed over and over again. Yet the most important thing that we have learned about her is that she has a passionate love for the Lord with all of her heart and she is a true follower and disciple of Jesus the Christ.

I love the clever title of this life impacting book **DIBBLE** meaning **Do It Blissfully Before Leaving Earth.** Dr. Henderson wastes no time in addressing what she calls the 3 powers in the earth. She very quickly grabs your attention on Life, Death and Choices. These three areas are clearly before hearts and minds at all times. **Dr. Henderson** brings attention, enlightenment, conviction and inspiration to these 3 areas from a biblical perspective.

DIBBLE accelerates to the great plan of salvation with all the details and wonderful benefits that are associated with this beautiful plan. Dr. Henderson's heart of love and concern is clearly expressed through her 7 simple steps that **guarantee**

heaven. Every reader will gain a greater insight and understanding from reading this life impacting book.

Dibble gets my thumbs up as a must read for both believers and unbelievers alike. She does a masterful job of breaking down the gospel and bringing clarity for those that may not truly understand the gospel message.

Dibble is an excellent choice and a must read. This is a book that will challenge your faith and cause you to examine your walk with the Lord.

I highly recommend this unique and well written book of truth to all that would like to look more deeply into the 3 powers of the Earth. Some of you will be refreshed and renewed in your spirit while others will be more challenged by the loving conviction of the Lord. All will be delighted and inspired by this powerful revelation of the truth. Jesus is coming soon!

Dr. James E. Randolph ACKGM Ministries Overseer

Introduction

I've been inspired to write this book D.I.B.B.L.E. "Do It Blissfully Before Leaving Earth" to enlighten you of the most important decisions that you will ever make in life. It's so important to enlighten yourself and seek knowledge of God, our creator, who is the source and beginning of all creation.

There are three powers on Earth: life, death, and choices. Life comes from God, who is the giver of all life. He breathed into man the breath of life and man became a living soul (Gen. 2:7). Death came from disobedience and sin. In the Garden of Eden, Adam and Eve made a "choice" to disobey God and the result was death for all mankind (Gen. 3:1–4).

We've all been given the power to make our own choices. We can't blame anyone else for the choices or decisions we make. Right now, you have the power to make a choice that will affect the rest of your life on Earth and heaven.

Thank God for the plan of Salvation through Jesus the Christ because now we have a choice to live eternally blissfully with Him in heaven forever. I use the word "blissfully" because it means in a manner characterized by extreme happiness or joy. Choosing God brings not just happiness, but *extreme* happiness.

Choice is what God gives to all mankind; everyone who has breath has choices. The Bible states "life or death ... choose life" (Deut. 30:19). Each day, we make decisions that will contribute to whether we live eternally with Jesus Christ blissfully, or eternal death with Satan in hell forever, where we are alive with feelings, emotions, and suffering.

Listen to what our Heavenly Father is saying in Deuteronomy 30:19: "This day I call the heavens and the earth as witnesses against you that I have set before you life and death, blessings and curses. Now choose life." He is stating heaven and Earth (all creation) are watching us as we make choices. He then gives us advice and states, "Choose life."

You may think everyone would choose life, but we don't, especially when we are young. We feel we are invincible and can do anything and won't have to pay the consequences. Think about it: making one bad choice can alter your whole life here on Earth and even in your afterlife. By making one wise choice to make Jesus, who is God, Lord of your life, can alter your entire life into a blissful journey to have eternal life in heaven.

We all have been given a God-given choice and He tells us to choose life. Why wouldn't we all choose life? Because of the sinful nature of our Earth suits and our deceitful hearts with which we were born. The Bible states, "The heart is deceitful above all things" (Jer. 19:9). We naturally think we know more than God.

My one and only son, Jamarr B. T., told me in the fifth grade that he knew more than I. He was so masculine and was determined to have everything the way that he desired. I laughed within and said to myself, "He has a lot to learn."

In reality, we feel this way about God and we all have a lot to learn. We never stop learning until we check out from Earth. I think we feel when we reach a certain level of maturity or age that we no longer need to continue to learn. With God, we are to continue to be humble like children and remain teachable: easy to forgive and easy to love.

Reality is, one day we all will check out from Earth because the Bible states it has been appointed once for man to die (Heb. 9:27). We all have an appointment with death just like we have appointments for everything. Choosing life brings blessings and choosing death brings curses. We can do this actively or passively. By existing and not actively preparing ourselves, we can make eternal decisions for our lives.

One day, death is going to occur for each of us. But, it's only the first death when our Earth suits are put six feet under. We simply transition in the spirit to the bosom of Abraham, or paradise, which leads to heaven or Hades (hell) or the grave, which leads to eternal death after leaving Earth. When we experience the death of a loved one, it appears that a person's life is over, but in reality, it's just beginning. We are all spirits and will live forever in a place that we've chosen before leaving Earth.

For those of you who can't move on after a death, look at their death as if they are gone on a long vacation and you will see them again if you chose to live a life in Christ and they've chosen a life with Christ. That important "dash", which is the life we live on Earth, will determine your fate and destiny. The present lifestyle you choose to live on Earth will determine where you will live eternally.

The Bible states "For God so loved the world that He gave his only begotten son, that whosoever believe in Him should not perish but have everlasting life" (John 3:16). Believing in Jesus will bring you an eternal blissful life!

DIBBLE explains seven simple steps to ensure you make it to heaven blissfully upon leaving Earth. Jesus is coming back soon and you must complete these seven steps to ensure you are heaven-bound! Once you leave Earth, it's not the end, but the beginning of where you will spend eternity: blissfully in heaven or eternally hell-bound.

Table of Contents

1

Choice One: Acknowledge God

There's nothing more important in life than acknowledging God, our Supreme Being. By acknowledging God, you will begin to know how important it is to intimately know and honor the one and only true God who created everything and everybody.

The greatest of the Ten Commandments found in Exodus 20:3 is, "Thou shalt have no other gods before me." It's easy to have other gods and put them before the omnipotent God. We ignorantly have many gods when we refuse to allow God to be number one in our lives. He must have first place or no place. He won't take second nor third place. It's easy to put everyone and everything before God. The way that we are made in our earth suits makes it easy to put people and things before God.

Our natural wants and desires are never fulfilled in our earth suits. When we begin to acknowledge God, we begin to shift from the natural to the spirit realm. Most of us think that we are just humans because of our senses, but we are all spirits that will live forever.

Proverbs 3:6 states, "in all your ways acknowledge God and He will direct your steps." What does that mean? It means we must recognize God as being in charge or ruler, and then we will begin to acknowledge His authority in whatever we choose to do daily. Remember He said acknowledge Him in all of our ways.

I reflect on when I was in college how I would first give God His time and ask His assistance with my assignments. Joyce Meyers had a radio ministry that I loved. I would receive my spiritual food every day, which was so good and helped me to focus. I would get A's every time on my assignments. I know I need God and He is greater than I and can work through me to execute the plans I have chosen if I acknowledge Him first.

I learned it's important that I seek God for His plans for my life because He has already planned our lives in heaven. Jeremiah 29:11 states, "'For I know the plans I have for you,' declares the Lord, 'plans to prosper you and not to harm you, plans to give you hope and a future.'" God already has our lives mapped out with plans to prosper us with hope and a future.

The key is we must acknowledge Him and allow Him to have preeminence in our choices. When you acknowledge Him, you can be sure there will be a manifestation of His presence in your life and the more that you allow Him, the more He will make His presence known.

If I don't acknowledge Him, it is possible that I may do well and ignorantly give myself credit for the gifts and talents He placed inside of me at birth. Yes, He gave us our gifts and talents when He formed us in our mother's womb.

To acknowledge is a continual process and as you continue to recognize Him relentlessly, He shows up in different areas of your life. God is always speaking, but are you listening? He has a still small voice (1 Kings 19:12). He desires for each and every one of us to give *Him* time to communicate with Him. He will speak back if we can be still and listen.

Prayer is a two-way conversation. Most of us just talk, talk, and talk to Him, but never wait on Him to answer or speak. He can speak through the Bible and also through an audible voice. Acknowledging God first needs to become a habit in our lives like brushing our teeth in order for everyone to know and fulfill our God-ordained purpose and be successful. It takes twenty-one days to make or break a habit. On day twenty-two, you will unconsciously continue or discontinue.

Acknowledging God is first, which entails allowing Him to order our steps which is essential in understanding how the Kingdom of God operates. This represents the invitation of believing in Jesus as God's Son and the process of possessing eternal life. We must learn how to live in the kingdom life God has given us through the power of acknowledging Him.

Remember everything we possess came from God, especially our gifts and talents from birth. Some of us who are gifted think we gave our gifts to ourselves. God creatively made each one of us and gave us our individual gifts and talents to complete the plans He began for us since the beginning of time.

Our lives have been already written in books in heaven. We agreed to the lives we are living in heaven as spiritual beings before we became humans on the earth. God carefully chose our mothers and fathers with the perfect DNA to complete His awesome plans of prosperity. None of us were mistakes, no matter how we arrived on planet Earth. In the Bible, He states in Jeremiah 1:5, "I knew you before you were formed in your mother's womb."

Acknowledging God is further explained in Colossians 3:17: "Whatsoever you do, whether in word or deed, do it in the name of the Lord." What does that mean, "do it in the name of the Lord"? Say the name as I do it? No. It means I do it on behalf of Him, giving Him the honor. I do it in place of Him. We are His hands and feet on the earth to use us as He pleases.

Whenever I am ministering or teaching, I say to myself, "How would Jesus say or explain this?" I speak and teach whatever it may be on His behalf.

Discipleship means learning to acknowledge God in all we do—and it takes a lot of learning. When Jesus began His ministry, He appointed twelve men to be disciples who turned the world upside down. Discipline means the practice of training people to obey rules, and using punishment to correct disobedience.

We all need discipline because of what happened in the Garden of Eden with Adam and Eve who chose to disobey God's rules. We never stop learning, which produces discipline because we are always learning, and increasingly we are able to acknowledge Him in all of our ways, not some of our ways.

During this process, we begin to die to our own will, and become more Christ-minded, and begin to do everything on behalf of the Lord Jesus the Christ. As we do that, among other things, our fear and anxiety disappear because we aren't out there on a limb by ourselves. These two twins, called "fear and anxiety", need to be eliminated from our lives. It's easily done as we acknowledge Him more. We are watching God in action doing great things in our lives.

The gospel states God accepts us where we are, because He puts us there. We are in the world to be the light of the world and the salt of the earth—and it is God who makes that possible. We must accept we are finite, we make mistakes, and no one is perfect. As we take a step back, we allow the work that God has appointed to flow through our lives as we become the person He intended us to be. God has high aims for you and me. His aim is for each one of us to become the kind of person He can empower to do whatever we desire to do. I must emphasize that you and I are being disciplined, trained, cultivated, and grown to the point where God can empower us to do what we both desire and want.

In this process, we must recognize a lot of work has to be in dying to ourselves or our "selfish list" before that can happen. This is what life is all about. We learn this as we deny ourselves and begin to learn to do as the disciples of Jesus Christ did. Paul, an apostle and disciple of Jesus Christ said, "It's not I but the Christ that lives in me" (Gal. 2:20). We become the twenty-first century disciples of Christ turning the world upside down and doing great things by acknowledging God and we will receive rewards in heaven (Matt. 5:12).

There is a price to pay for suffering with the blessings. I know you don't want to hear this because who wants to suffer? However, remember that we all suffer in life through afflictions and trouble in the earth. "A man's life is of a few days full of trouble" (Job 14:1).

Without God, nothing would exist, especially not you nor me. In the beginning, God created the heaven and the earth (Gen. 1:1) and in Genesis 1:27, He created man and woman in His image. In the beginning was the Word, and the Word was with God and the Word (Jesus) became flesh and dwelt among us and the Word is God (John 1:1). God, a spirit, wrapped Himself in flesh like us as His Son Jesus, enabling us to see Him and touch Him.

Many people don't understand the godhead, but it's simple: just as we can't separate ourselves being spirit and flesh, we can't separate God who is a spirit and manifested Himself physically in the flesh as Jesus. Spirit is invisible and flesh allows us to physically see the natural.

Jesus, our perfect example, always acknowledged His Father God as He experienced everything in His human life. He experienced everything that we experience in life and endured everything we endure with all of the limitless temptations yet without sinning. He showed us how to acknowledge God and how to live a purpose-driven life victoriously. Even in His brutal death on the cross, He taught us how to suffer and forgive each other. He stated, "Father, forgive them for they do not know not what they are doing" (Luke 23:34). Jesus looked down from the cross upon a scene that must have been stressful and embarrassing to Him.

We all have stressful and embarrassing moments in our lives, but maybe not to the intensity that Jesus suffered. Let's take a look at the awesome plan of salvation Jesus suffered and endured just for us and teaching us all at the same time how to acknowledge God.

The Roman soldiers were gambling for Jesus' clothing (John 19:24) and the criminals on the cross on both sides made Jesus look like a criminal too. One of them was reviling Him, probably saying, "If you are who you say you are, do something" (Matt. 27:44). The Roman soldiers were busy and greedy, gambling for His clothes while the religious leaders were mocking Him (Matt. 27:41–43). The crowd was blaspheming Him. Throughout all of this intensity, humiliation, and unworthy lot, Jesus, our great intercessor, prayed, "Father, forgive them." Oh, what great love and mercy! Remember, He was teaching us what to do when the people we love and strangers (enemies) hurt us and do unspeakable acts of unkindness to us.

Even in His agony, Jesus' concern was for the forgiveness of those who counted themselves among His enemies. He asked the Father to forgive the one thief on the cross who foolishly jeered at Him. He asked the Father to forgive the Roman soldiers who had mocked Him, spit on Him, beat Him, yanked out His beard, whipped Him, put a crown of thorns on His head, and nailed Him to the cross. Jesus asked forgiveness for the angry mob that had mocked Him and demanded that He be crucified (Mark 15:29–30). The mob included His own chosen people who hated Him the most.

It is important to note that Jesus' prayer, as He was acknowledging our only wise God, "Father, forgive them," does not mean everyone was forgiven, unilaterally, without repentance and individual faith. This is an important fact that we shouldn't ever forget. The two most important components of salvation are repentance and faith in God because without faith, it's impossible to please Him (Heb. 11:6). Oh, but forgiveness is the main ingredient in the plan of salvation which occurs when we begin to acknowledge Him, because if we don't forgive each other, then God won't forgive us. Believe me, we all need forgiveness because we easily sin in our words, by lying, in deeds, our actions, and thoughts.

As we take a step back and look at Jesus, it intensely illustrates how Jesus was willing to forgive them—forgiveness was, in fact, the reason He was on the cross. The words "Father, forgive them" show how Jesus manifested as God in the flesh and showed the merciful heart of God our Father. Oh, acknowledging God will manifest in you as you begin to desire to possess a forgiving heart. We must embrace this powerful act.

Jesus prayed, "Father, forgive them," because He was powerfully fulfilling the Old Testament prophecy: "He bore the sin of many (all of us), and made intercession (took our place) for the transgressors" (all of us) (Isa. 53:12). From the cross, Jesus interceded for sinners. Today, risen and glorified, Jesus remains the "one mediator between God and mankind" (1 Tim. 2:1). Jesus prayed, "Father, forgive them" because He was putting into practice the principle He had taught in the wonderful Sermon on the Mount. "You have heard that it was said, 'Love your neighbor and hate your enemy.' But, I tell you, love your enemies and pray for those who persecute you" (Matt. 5:43–44) is key for life. Jesus, the great teacher, "the persecuted", prayed for His persecutors. This is a tough lesson to learn in the natural, but with Jesus, it becomes easier.

Jesus, wrapped up in flesh as God, our Father, was coupled with the willingness to forgive His tormentors which is the fact that "they did not know what they were doing" (Luke 23:34). The sinners who put Jesus on the cross were ignorant of the truth of their actions, just as we are at times. Just saying you don't know won't be an excuse.

The soldiers personally held no ill will toward Jesus. They were simply following orders. This was how they normally treated condemned men, and they believed He truly deserved it. It appeared that Jesus was guilty. They didn't know that they were killing the Son of God, named Jesus.

The mob didn't know whom they were trying to destroy. The Jewish leaders had deceived them into believing that Jesus was a fake (a "perpetrator" is the word our youth uses frequently today), and a troublemaker (Acts 3:17).

The millennials know or recognize a perpetrator a mile away. They aren't easily deceived. They are looking for the real thing. There's nothing like the real thing and Jesus is the real thing.

The whole plan of salvation with Jesus on the cross is about forgiveness. In praying, as Jesus was acknowledging God, said, "Father, forgive them," which revealed His infinite mercy. He still loved them and would forgive them if only they would humble themselves and repent. It takes humbleness to repent, which is being godly sorrowful.

Jesus' prayer "Father, forgive them" was answered in the lives of many people. The Roman centurion at the foot of the cross, upon seeing how Jesus died, exclaimed, "Surely this man was the Son of God!" (Mark 15:39).

One of the two thieves crucified with Jesus exercised faith in Christ, who promised him paradise (Luke 23:39–43). A member of the Sanhedrin named Nicodemus publicly aligned himself with Jesus and offered assistance (John 19:39). And, a little over a month later, three thousand people in Jerusalem were saved in one day as the church began (Acts 2:4). This was supernatural. The great awakening had begun. Jesus even fed thousands after He taught them. He was so thoughtful and caring.

On the cross, Jesus acknowledged our Heavenly Father and provided forgiveness for all of us who would ever believe in Him (Matt. 20:28). Jesus paid the penalty for the sins that we commit in our ignorance, and even the ones we've committed deliberately. Yes we are all sinners before we become His children. When we are born again, we, too, become an answer to Jesus' prayer of, "Father, forgive them." We must all follow Jesus' example.

As Jesus talked with Nicodemus prior to the crucifixion, He said:

> "I tell you the truth, no one can see the kingdom of God unless he is born again."

> "How can a man be born when he is old?" Nicodemus asked. "Surely he cannot enter a second time into his mother's womb to be born!"

> Jesus answered, "I tell you the truth, no one can enter the kingdom of God unless he is born of water and the Spirit. Flesh gives birth to flesh,

but the Spirit gives birth to spirit. You should
not be surprised at my saying, 'You must be
born again.'"(John 3:3–7)

This includes all of us. This process begins simply when we
acknowledge and ask Jesus to become Lord of our lives. The
plan of salvation is so simple, an imbecile or idiot can do it.

It's a choice to acknowledge and love God. Choose to
acknowledge and love will follow and if you truly love God,
you will obey Him. Sometimes it may be difficult to obey Him
and the things He ordained that we suffer, but the brighter side
is that it will work out for your good if you choose to remain
faithful to God.

In God we live, move, and have our being or existence
(Acts 17:28). Every experience or activity we participate in is
because of the life and breath given to us from the almighty
God. God creatively created everything and everyone for
Himself. He made mankind for Himself so that we can
acknowledge and worship Him. Worship means having the
feeling or expression of reverence and adoration for a deity
who is God.

Even when Adam sinned, God knew this and had a plan of
salvation so that we can all spend eternity with Him in heaven.
The plan of salvation of Jesus living on Earth and enduring all
of our temptations but never sinning is for all of us to escape
eternal death. He endured the shame of the cross and was res-
urrected from the dead.

In case you didn't know, it was embarrassing being on that
cross with thieves. It looked like he was guilty too. But, in the
invisible spirit realm, He was busy in hell, conquering death,
hell, and the grave so that we could have everlasting life (1
Cor.15:55–57). Revelation 1:18 states, "I am he that live and

was dead; and behold, I am alive forevermore, Amen, and have keys of hell and of death."

Everlasting life replaces eternal death. Did you read that with understanding? Jesus, who died and arose from the dead, went into the spirit realm and victoriously took the keys of hell and death from the devil and through Him we can all have everlasting life.

I reflect of the artist Chaka Chan, a believer who sang "Everlasting Love." I see her singing on behalf of God. God wants to give us everlasting love so we can have everlasting life. I always loved that song and thought it was about people giving each other everlasting love and we can only do this with Christ. Her song gives you a taste of love through her beautiful music.

God, through Jesus, shows us how to love, live, and acknowledge Him. He became acquainted with our griefs and pains. These are more twins in life that we all experience. We all have griefs (disappointments) and pains (problems). The Bible says in Job 14:16 that a man's life is of a few days and full of trouble. The instant a new baby makes his first cry, trouble begins. He is hungry and has many needs. It continues with all of us as we reach maturity in life, whatever our age may be.

We all need to acknowledge God. God created a hole in everyone's' heart and only He can fill it. We may try to fill it with money, food, wine, sex, pleasure etc., but only God brings true fulfillment. He is the only answer for the world today. Nobody and nothing can fulfill you like God. In His presence is fullness of joy and at his right hand pleasures forevermore (Psalm 16:11). Everyone desires joy and pleasure. More twins which makes life worth the living! It's yours for the asking when you acknowledge Him.

Choose to acknowledge and make Him Lord and King of your life! It's a choice. Acknowledging God means you need

Him. You will experience the greatest joy of your life in this process, and you will learn to love Him and if you truly love God, you will obey Him with bliss. It's a sure thing.

2

Choice Two: Choose To Accept God

Accepting God entails letting go of your will and allowing God to lead and guide you entirely. By doing this, you will begin to allow God to rule in your life. The Bible says, "Let God arise" (Ps. 68:1). In other words, let God drive.

We all know two people can't drive a car at once. This means you must move out of the driver's seat and allow God to drive and listen to Him. We must let God rule or be in charge. Don't contend with God and continue to put your two cents in about how you want to do this or that.

When we are young we are full of ourselves. Learn to be still and quiet and take time to learn. Just like the word "ear" is in the center of the word "heart", you must begin to listen with your heart, which is also in the center of your chest. The heart is naturally deceitful (Jer. 17:9), so we need the heart of God living in us. Believe me, He knows what's best for you. Not only that, He knows your beginning, everything in between, and your ending. He is omniscient, which means all knowing; omnipotent, which means all powerful; and omnipresent, which means everywhere at the same time.

He's our supernatural Father who delights in blessing His children. He will not force you to accept Him. He is a gentleman. He will wait patiently to draw those who will allow

Him a place in their life. Since He's all-knowing, He already knows who will and who won't submit and allow Him a place.

When it's your time to check out from Earth, it's of utmost importance that you have accepted Jesus as your Savior. It's too late after you have checked out! The Bible states, "For one not to harden his heart when God himself knocks at our hearts" (Heb. 3:15). He actually knocks on our hearts. He already knows who will and won't accept Him. He wishes that no man be damned and go to hell, but He already knows who will and who won't, and believe it or not, He knows us better than we know ourselves.

The hole, which is a void, that everyone has in their heart, God created it for Him and only Him. He is the only one who can bring true happiness. By accepting God as your Savior, you may live forever in heaven in eternal blissfulness. Everyone on Earth needs to accept Jesus, who was the ultimate sacrifice; He is the only door which will allow everyone to enter into heaven.

Choosing to go to heaven is a choice. After we leave Earth, our souls will go to either heaven or hell. The Bible states that the soul that sins will die and this is an eternal death (Ezek. 18:20). It also says to work out your soul salvation with fear and trembling, which means to attentively plan your life according to God's Word, which is the Bible. The Bible is your roadmap for life. God made human beings and we didn't evolve from apes. Stop fighting God. He knows what's best for you. Accept Him and let Him be in charge and order your footsteps!

Just as a wise man's footsteps are ordered by God (Ps. 27:33), accept Him today. Nobody knows what the future holds for us but God. It's simple: decide today by simply asking Jesus to be Lord of your life. It is accepting the gift of eternal life. It's not Burger King, where you can have your way. In the kingdom of God, it's God's way. Your arms are too short to box with God.

You will be so happy and blissful, and true peace will join you. Begin by praying the prayer below:

Pray:

- Dear God, I am a sinner and need your forgiveness. I believe Jesus Christ shed His precious blood and died for my sin. I am willing to change and turn from my sin. I now invite Jesus Christ to come into my heart and life as my personal Savior.

  "But as many as received him, to them He gave power to become the sons of God, even to them that believe on His name." (John 1:12)

  "Therefore if any man be in Christ, he is a new creature: old things are passed away; behold all things are become new [new life begins]." (2 Cor. 5:17)

3

Choice Three: Choose to Prosper and Be in Good Health

W e should all choose to live each day to its fullest and to prosper in all that we do. It's natural that we all want to prosper in life. The Bible says: "Above all, I wish that ye prosper and be in good health even as your soul prospers" (3 John 2). "Prosper" comes from the word "prosperity", which means a place of continual blessings. Blessing means being continually happy. It's a choice. Jesus died so that we may have life and it more abundantly. It is stated that the wealth of the wicked is stored up for you from God (Prov. 13:22).

I believe that it's waiting in a physical or spiritual storehouse just for you and me. You must seek God for your stored-up blessings.

I believe we have bank accounts in heaven that we can access on Earth through the spiritual realm through faith. We all have been born with a measure of faith, which I call a faith muscle. By beginning to exercise your faith muscle, which entails believing in Jesus, it can surely begin to happen. You must seek God for your stored-up blessings in faith in order to prosper.

We all believe and have faith in something. Choose to have faith in God and make Him your source and you will begin to prosper. It's important to make sure your soul prospers. Your soul is the essential part of you, which consists of your will and emotions, what makes you happy or sad. It is the part of you that makes decisions. Simultaneously, you will prosper in your plans as your soul prospers. It happens twofold in faith through your choices.

Strive for good health. This entails striving for godly and good habits. We all need godly appetites. God desires that we have good health. We are creatures of habit. It takes twenty-one days to make or break a habit. This means on day twenty-two, you will do whatever it is without thinking about it!

You are what you eat. We feed our natural man every day because our stomachs tell us every day. In the Bible, the question is asked: is your stomach your God (Phil. 3:19)? I laugh because when I first attempted to fast at my church "Logan Park" in Gary, IN under the leadership of Bishop George Stearnes, I would smell barbeque in the air and I would stop and break my fast because surely, my stomach was my god and in charge. I'm thankful that I'm stronger today and my spirit man has matured more. Some of us are mature in age and are babies in the spirit. Vice versa, some children are mature spiritual beings.

We are spirits and live in a temporary body and will one day leave to live eternally with God or eternally in hell with the devil. It's your choice. The Bible says, "Choose ye this day whom you will serve, man or God." Choosing to serve God will bring prosperity. Choosing to prosper entails choosing who you will serve and obey. Serving man will lead to eternal death. It's easy to be a man-pleaser by simply doing nothing but what we feel like doing. Choosing to prosper involves choosing to be a God-pleaser, which means seeking to please and obey Him.

When we seek to please God, He will lead us in every way. He will dictate our habits. Remember, He desires that we prosper and be in good health even as our soul prospers. Being in good health can lead to wealth or prosperity. To be in good health both naturally and spiritually, both must work together simultaneously as we allow God to be in charge. We need to be sold out to God and speak like Paul in the Bible, who said, "it's no longer I but the Christ that lives in me" (Gal. 2:20).

Our power comes from God living within us and allowing Him full reign. God doesn't want us lukewarm (Rev. 3:16), trying to serve God and the devil at the same time, not fully surrendering. Being fully submitted will lead to full prosperity.

My son, Jamarr Booker T., said some people are twenty-four hours, seven days a week God-pleasers. He laughingly told my daughter Binika that Mom is one. My other daughter Jazz said, "No, I think you are twenty-five hours or more." I laughed within.

I feel we all should choose to be twenty-four hours a day, seven days a week God-pleasers.

Prospering and being in good health are what we all desire and they will occur the blissful, godly way, which is the best way to possess eternal life.

4

Choose to Be "Blessed" (Happy)

D ecide to be blessed or happy. Kirk Franklin and Pharrell Williams both have songs about being *happy*. They were both big hits and everyone danced and sang them. "Blessed" in the Bible means "a favor or gift bestowed by God, thereby bringing happiness or the invoking of God's favor upon a person's life."

Favor from God comes from the word "grace", which is God's unmerited favor. We do nothing to receive it. Grace comes from God when we choose to accept Him as our Savior.

Remember choice is one of the greatest powers we possess in life. We choose to be blessed. The flip side is, it's also a choice to choose to be cursed. We make choices and can't blame anyone else when we are tempted. The Bible states in Deuteronomy 3, "blessings or curses, you choose."

Our choices become life-altering experiences. One bad choice can alter the course of your life. You might say, "I only choose to be blessed." Who would choose to curse themselves? It's happening every day.

Being blessed means you will allow God to be Lord of your life. He will help you to direct your thoughts. Thoughts may enter our minds daily, but it's up to us what we entertain. The Bible states we are to "think about things which are lovely, just, and of a good report, if there be any virtue, if there be any praise, we are to think about these things" (Phil. 4:8). We need to be determined to think about good things and make our minds behave. The Bible says to have the mind of Christ. It's a choice. Your mind needs discipline and control. Your mind has a mind of its own. It spins out of control—especially with all of the technical gadgets and distractions we have today. Just try for a minute to meditate on something. Your mind can take you all over the world in seconds. But, if we ask God to help us, He will. He is a gentleman. He won't do it unless we ask Him. Talk to your mind and *choose* to live a life of blessings, happiness, and discipline.

Choose to be blessed by God because the devil imitates God. He tempted Jesus to worship him. He appears as an angel of light. He may look like the real thing, but he isn't. God gives basic instructions on how to live in this world and be blessed: "Do not be conformed to this world, but be transformed by the renewal of your mind, that by testing you may discern what is the will of God, what is good and acceptable and perfect" (Rom. 12:2).

The devil will bring temporary happiness through temporary things. He is a liar and a great deceiver. He tricks us if we choose to serve him, and he will give you everything on Earth that is temporal. If you choose to worship and obey him, the end is eternal death.

Don't look at the world and how the wicked people prosper because it may cause you to choose to live a luxury life of sin. Sin has pleasure for a season. The devil tempted Jesus and gave Him his own Word from the Bible. He told Him if He worshiped him, he would give Him the kingdoms of the earth (Matt. 4:1–11). He is the pseudo-ruler of the earth and thinks he owns it but everything truly belongs to God.

The Bible tells us to love not the world nor the things of it (1 John 2:15–17). True happiness only comes from choosing to love and obey God and happiness will be a sure benefit full of His blessings and promises. The promises, which are the blessings of the Lord, are "Yes" and "Amen" (2 Cor. 1:20). The promises will bring happiness. The blessing of the Lord, it makes one rich, and He adds no sorrow with it (Prov. 10:22). The blessings of God will make you rich both naturally and spiritually and without sorrow. We know that people who are rich naturally are not immune to sorrow. All worldly things bring care and sorrow. The spiritual realm of God's blessings is without sorrow.

Choosing to be blessed yields great results and benefits. One great benefit in the Bible is: "But seek first His kingdom and His righteousness, and all these things will be added to you" (Matt. 6:33). By choosing God and a blessed life will automatically add all of the other things we desire.

We learn from the Bible how to live following the process in 2 Peter 1:5–7, which states:

> For this very reason, make every effort to supplement your faith with virtue, and virtue with knowledge, and knowledge with self-control, and self-control with steadfastness, and steadfastness with godliness, and godliness with brotherly affection, and brotherly affection with love.

Never forget about love because God is love. It's the greatest power in earth and heaven. It's a package deal when you choose to accept God and choose to be blessed.

Yet, we must choose to walk in love, especially with the unlovable people who may be some of your family members. It's a choice, and with the help of the Lord, we even learn to love our enemies.

When blessings come, enemies increase because of jealousy. There isn't a need to be jealous when we all have an equal chance with God because He isn't a respecter of persons. He loves us all individually, as different as we all are. Blessings accompany equal opportunities, which are available as we all pay our dues. "In all toil there is profit" (Prov. 14:23).

Choosing to be blessed by God will even bring rewards in the afterlife in heaven. God has high purposes for obedient children. Obedience brings blessings. It is advantageous to learn to be quick to obey. When we fully obey God, blessings will chase us down. God looks down from heaven to see who He can trust to greatly bless. We must fully obey, and big blessings, opportunities, and prosperity are everywhere we go and in everything we do. In 2 Chronicles 20:20 states believe in the Lord and He will establish you, believe in his prophets and you will prosper. In my church, Advancing Christ Kingdom Global Ministries, overseers, Apostle James and Prophetess Sharon Randolp flow in prophesy and apostolic power. I know pesonally if you believe in God and in the prophets first hand, you will be established and prosper because the bible states it.

Kirk Franklin wrote, "Wanna be Happy" and "Smile. Pharrell wrote "Happy." These songs sold millions of copies. I interceded for God to save the rappers, and God saved Kanye West. I love his new Album "Jesus Is Born". The song I play each morning is "Count Your Blessings". This is something we all should do! By doing this, the blessings will continue to surely flow, and you will be happy. Nobody wants us to be happy more than God. No one can truly be happy without God.

Jesus came that we may have life and it more abundantly (John 10:10). It may happen or it may not—it's all up to us. Choose to be blessed, happy, and live a blissful life of abundance.

5

Choose to be Diligent in Seeking God

Isaiah 5:6–7 states, "Seek the Lord while He may be found; Call upon Him while He is near. Let the wicked forsake his way and the unrighteous man his thoughts; and let him return to the Lord, and He will have compassion on him." We must intentionally try to seek God when He can be found, which means there are times when He can't be found. God initially draws us to Him.

I can remember working in Chicago as a computer operator at Sargent and Lundy Engineers when my children were small. I was earning a substantial amount of money and considered myself blessed. I was satisfied and as I was walking to the train, I had an important conversation with God. I asked Him, "What happens when we achieve the things we desire in life and then die? Is that all there is to life? When we die, is that the end?"

At that moment, God began to draw me to Him. Everywhere I went for entertainment began to be God-centered. I went bowling and it was a Gospel night at the bowling alley. This continued often. It happened so often that I began to seek God and He began to draw me closer to Him. It was amazing as I reminisced on how I began my natural process of enjoying life and the events began to draw my spiritual person even closer to God. As I sought God the more, He used my sister Miriam from Milwaukee, who greatly interceded for me, and while I was visiting her, I was filled with the precious gift of the Holy Ghost at her church. She continued in prayer for me to be led to a church that was teaching the truth. (John 1:17 For the law was given through Moses; grace and truth came through Jesus Christ). I was so hungry for the truth that my sweet friend Pat and I bought tons of bibles and study references and every Saturday we diligently studied for hours and hours seeking to know more!

Whenever I had questions God would supernaturally have my cousins Gwen and Ethel to buy books for me exactly with the answers I needed. I would not tell them when I was coming in town, but they stated God told them when I was coming and told them what books to buy. God loves it when we seek Him.

My husband had a friend whom he was fond of who had a friend named Joyce who was strategically used to draw me to a church called Logan Park Assembly of Christ in Gary, IN under the leadership of Dr. Bishop George Stearnes for prayer. Joyce along with Sharla and Vincent were phenomenal as God used them to assist Him in laying a good spiritual foundation for my life for which I am extremely grateful.

Debrah my play sister from First A.M.E. Church joined Logan Park too, and we both soared higher as we sought the Lord.

While seeking God for my purpose, He confirmed my healing ministry along with Leona and Darlene P. as we were used in powerful demonstrations of God's supernatural healing power.

God continued to set up supernatural healing encounters that I extremely enjoyed. Sharla had a friend who was paralyzed from a car accident, and she asked me to come to the hospital to pray for him. I prayed and he felt heat as I laid my hand on his legs. She told me that he walked out of the hospital the next day! Leona and I went to the hospital to see a Sister Pam who had transitioned. We prayed her back to life and a tear came out of her eye and she did not desire to return. We also prayed and laid hands on Sister Sharon who had a tumor in her breast and prior to scheduled surgery, the Xray revealed God had removed the tumor!

Even my children and grandchildren experienced powerful supernatural encounters. Seeking God even more led to such heavenly beautiful supernatural experiences with Miriam and Sharla that reminded me of the show by Sid Roth's "Its Supernatural".

As I reminisce of a supernatural experience, I was praying and seeking for God to supernaturally heal my beautiful Madea Ermine Morris, but instead the Lord blessed my mom Dollie, Madea, and I with a beautiful supernatural vision before she transitioned to heaven. God is full of supernatural surprises when seeking Him!

Prayer is conversation with God. If we are quiet, He speaks back in a still, small voice or His Word, the Bible. God will also use His prophets to speak into our lives (2 Chron. 20:20). This is a part of the seeking process. Most of us just pour out our hearts in prayer but never ask God His thoughts for us, nor sit still long enough to hear His response. Remember prayer is a conversation and a two-way dialogue. It is essential that you diligently spend quality time with God.

By diligently seeking God, you will begin to see the benefits of prayer and the blessings of seeking God. This process leads to prospering and wealth, which leads to delightfulness. The Bible states if we delight ourselves in God, He will give us the desires of our hearts (Ps. 37:4). This is the fruit of being diligent.

Seeking is a process. It's like when a man is seeking for his wife. He is adamant about finding his sweet thing. Did you know God is sweeter than the honey in the honeycomb (Ps. 119:103)? The Bible says to taste and see that the Lord is good; blessed or happy is the man that trust in Him (Ps. 34:8). A man is supposed to trust God to find his wife. Just seek and try God, and get a taste of Him, and you will begin to see how blissful it is.

As your diligent relationship of seeking God enhances, you will begin to establish a trust in God. Trusting will bring true happiness. As He brings true happiness, He will give you the desires of your heart, which means you don't have to ask Him.

Early in my marriage, I wanted a new car. I only told God about it. One day, my husband said, "Let's go buy you a new car." I was so happy and began to see the price of being diligent pays. What a reward! Just be diligent and delight yourself and promises of God will manifest. The promises of God are "Yes" and "Amen", which means that settles it (2 Cor. 1:20).

We all are diligently seeking someone or something in life to make us happy both passively and actively. It's your choice to make sure you seek God first and that God has first place on the throne of your heart. If we allow Him to have first place, He will ensure our dreams, projects, and plans manifest at His ordained time. Remember timing is all up to God. Many times, we miss the promises because we stop believing or waiting. The Bible states, "Wait on the Lord and be of good courage, and again I say, wait on the Lord" (Ps. 27:14). Patience which is the capacity to accept or tolerate delay is a fruit of the spirit from God.

Because God is a rewarder of those that diligently seek Him, all of the things we desire are already done by Him in faith. We all love rewards when we have completed a great project. The reward of a finished project is oh so lovely.

Begin seeking God by trying to make an appointment to spend uninterrupted time with Him. We make appointments daily for everything and everybody. We all have an appointment with death. It's only the first death, because after we leave Earth, the eternal death in hell will surely occur if you haven't made the decision to invite God to be Lord of your life. Because, when we all leave planet Earth, it's simply a transition. We instantly leave Earth and are either in the presence of God in paradise or in the presence of the devil in Hell. Just as we make appointments in the natural, we can miss death's appointment too.

There are two Bible characters that experienced this phenomenal event. Elijah, a prophet from the Bible who performed many miracles, was carried away to heaven in a chariot of fire (2 Kings 2:3–9). Enoch was a man who walked with God, which means he had such an intimate relationship that God took him away supernaturally to heaven (Gen. 5:21–24). Hezekiah was told to get his house in order, which was his earthy business because it was time for him to die or transitioned. He asked God for fifteen additional years and God gave it to him. He was able to delay his death (2 Kings 20:1–7). These men sought God diligently and had supernatural experiences with God. Seeking diligently opens the supernatural realm.

The Rapture is a supernatural act where the Lord will blow His trumpet and the people who died with the Lord as their Savior will all supernaturally leave from their graves. Next, we who are alive and remain shall be caught up supernaturally to meet the Lord in the sky and so shall we forever be with Him

(1 Thess. 4:16–18). These individuals will escape death while living on Earth. I desire to be one of them. I get excited every time I think about it. The time is drawing closer to the return of our Savior Jesus Christ.

Diligently seeking God, who is supernatural, will birth the supernatural experiences because you have chosen to allow Him to live in you. We naturally enjoy the supernatural heroes at the movies. Just imagine how blissful your supernatural life will be by diligently seeking God. We all are natural human beings and spirits and can enjoy having a blissful supernatural experience while living on Earth. This is the fruit of being diligent.

6

Choose to Have Faith in God

Faith is the substance of things hoped for and the evidence of things not seen (Heb. 11:1). This means faith is made of things we dream or plans we desire to manifest physically but it begins as invisible on Earth. By having faith or believing in God and His Son Jesus, you will receive the reward of eternal life (John 3:16). We all have been given the measure of faith at birth (Rom. 12:3).

The faith process begins as a hope and a dream and escalates to proof right before your eyes. The elements of faith are preparation and expectation. Both require *action*, which brings a demonstration, which is what I call the "proof in the pudding." Just as a pregnant lady in faith prepares and buys items for her unborn baby, we must actively prepare for the Lord to return spiritually in faith.

We are spirits, which means we will live forever. We are living in a body, our "earth suits", and possess a soul that entails our will, emotions, and decisions or control center. We often let our bodies be in control instead of our spirit-man because of our senses. Our bodies, which are composed of lust and strong passions, like to rule, but instead, our spirit-man should be in charge. This can only occur with discipline. Discipline, defined by Webster, is the practice of training people to obey rules or a code of behavior; using punishment to correct disobedience.

We must learn to deny our natural man with discipline to help to develop the spirit to be the ruler and develop our faith muscle.

We all are born with a measure of faith, a muscle. If you never do anything with your faith muscle, you won't ever know it's there. It takes discipline to develop your faith muscle, which begins with just believing.

You should begin to try to have faith in God because we easily put our faith in people and objects without any effort. Without faith, it's impossible to please God (Heb. 11:6). Remember, we all have the measure of faith, which came with us at birth (Rom. 12:3). I don't believe we all have the same measure of faith because God's plan varies for each of us. The Bible states if we have the faith the size of a mustard seed, which is the smallest seed God created, we can move mountains (Luke 17:6).

We all have been carefully formed according to the DNA from our parents to be exactly what God has planned for us in life. By having faith in God, He will reveal the secrets of His plans to you individually (Deut. 29:29). The Bible is our roadmap for life. Everything we need for our destiny is in it. We have faith in objects, such as chairs we sit in, people we love, houses we buy, and money, which the Bible states answers all things (Eccl. 10:19). I guess this is why man desires money so much. There is nothing wrong with having money, but the Bible says the love of money is the root of all evil (1 Tim. 6:10). Loving money too much can open the doors to all kinds of evil actions. The Bible says it's difficult for a rich man to enter the kingdom of heaven because he will have faith in his money more than faith in God (Matt. 19:24).

For those of you who are rich in houses and land, you must begin to allow God in your heart and trust Him as He guides you with your wealth. God gives man the power to obtain wealth (Deut. 8:18). Sometimes it may be difficult to have faith in God, which entails trusting and obeying Him first, but it will always turn out for our good as long as we are on God's page. The Bible says, "If we believe (have faith) in our hearts and confess with our mouth that Jesus is Lord who is God, we will receive eternal life and live in heaven forever." This takes *faith*.

What we do while living on Earth, which is that all-powerful "dash" between the day you were born and the day you die, determines where we will live eternally. Remember we are spirits and will live forever. It's your choice where you will spend eternity. Use your own measure of faith individually to first trust and obey and have faith in God in your journey of life. Faith entails trusting, and once you begin to trust, you will learn to obey His still small voice. Sometimes you may not obey because we are accustomed to trusting our own minds. This will take faith exercises. When you make a mistake, repent or tell God you are sorry and try again. It's such a joy to exercise your faith muscle. The more you believe, the more faith you acquire in God, thus the more you will receive. Your faith muscle will have the same intensity as when you begin to exercise your physical muscle.

It is necessary to connect with God to find out the good plans He has for you. The Bible says, "Only what we do for Christ will last" (1 Cor. 15:58). It's impossible to please God without faith. We have no excuse because He has given us everything we need to accomplish His will and His plan. Make up your mind to use that measure of faith for God which will birth great accomplishments.

I think of Oprah Winfrey, whom I consider to be a great woman of faith. She continues to soar higher and higher with her faith muscle. Anything Oprah endorses turns to gold. What a life! It's amazing to keep dreaming, believing, and receiving.

Another powerful minister of God is Joyce Meyers, who inspired me during my early years of salvation with her tremendous teachings on faith that are so life applicable.

We also need faith to love and obey God. We are all commanded to love God with all of our heart, mind, soul, and strength and love our neighbors like we love ourselves (Luke 10:27). That's a lot of loving. The Bible states all things work together for the good of those who love God and are called according to His purpose or plans (Rom. 8:28). Did you notice the word "God" is in the word "good"? There's no good without God. Pay attention to His purposes and His plans and make them have preeminence in your life.

Not everyone loves God; therefore you aren't called according to His purpose, which means you aren't fulfilling your God-fulfilling purpose. We all are naturally self-centered and are only concerned about our own plans and purposes. This is the way we all are before we ask God to be Lord of our lives. God must be a part of your life and have first place in your life. He is a jealous God, and won't have second place. It's the Kingdom of God's way where He is King of kings and Lord of lords! Again, by confessing with our mouths and believing with our hearts that He is Lord (Rom. 10:9), we begin the first stage of the process for a God-focused life, which is the beginning of a brand-new life, being born-again with faith. It's a new attitude, mindset, and direction. You are a brand-new person with a brand-new life. Everything is new. You must begin to exercise your faith muscle. If you don't exercise it, you won't be able to execute God's plans for your life. The Bible says to examine yourself to see if you are still in faith (2 Cor. 13:5). This means you need to take a good look at your life and see if you are still actively believing and producing what God has ordained for your life.

My husband, Booker T. II carried his weights around in the trunk of his car when I first met him. He was serious about developing his physical body and muscles. I can still see him proudly flexing his muscles to me over forty years ago. I was impressed. He looked awesome! It took discipline, diet, exercise, and patience to obtain an excellent physique. My son-in-love, Terrance, began developing his muscles after he married my daughter, DarNieshia. He began with discipline, diet, exercise, and patience. You should see him today. He is the epitome of a perfect physique and is training my twin grandsons. My daughter loves him so much. He's a minister, so he knows it takes momentum both ways to physically and spiritually develop his natural muscles and his faith muscle. My son, Jamarr Booker T., is developing his physical and faith muscles too. He is a minister too. Remember, in the natural, it took discipline, diet, exercise, and patience for them to develop their bodies into beautiful muscles and physiques.

In the spirit, it takes discipline, diet, exercise, and patience to develop your faith muscle. Discipline entails having a mind to do whatever it takes to have the finished product of the project. We all have different products that will require a plan with goals. We need discipline to begin and finish the process to produce the ideal product. Our diet must be inclusive of the Word of God, praying, and being surrounded by people of God praying. Diet means we must feed our spirit mind to stay focus and not partake in activities that can hinder or distract from seeing the manifestation of the finished product. Little distractions will take one off course and it may be difficult to get back on. You must feed your mind Bible scriptures or quotes for whatever you are trying to produce. Exercise is hearing and rehearsing the Word of God, and continuing to fight the good fight of faith. Exercise is needed to keep you in faith believing that it will happen no matter how long it takes, which is where patience kicks in. I've heard many people say, "I believed for ten years or more", and then they stopped believing. I asked them why they stopped believing. Remember, you will need to possess perseverance to pursue your dream and continue, no matter how long it takes.

I had a dream to open the first charter school in Merrillville, Indiana, which I named HIAT (Heritage Institute of Arts and Technology, now called Higher Institute of Arts and Technology). "Heritage" because the Bible says, "Children are a heritage; the fruit of the womb is God's reward" (Ps. 127:3).

It all began while attending a prayer breakfast given by Gary Educators for Christ when Dr. Mildred C. Harris, the overseer and a mother of Zion prophesied that I would open a school twenty years before I began my faith journey of pursuing HIAT, which actually began in the year of 2009. God even had me to teach in the same schools I attended in Gary, Indiana, which was the best school corporation in the US. Every teacher had to have a Master's Degree. My mom, Dollie L. Adamson, daughter of John & Azirlee Frazier, an educator of Gary Schools, and magna cum laude of Shorter College in Arkansas, was by my side teaching me the rudiments of life in faith from knee high to an adult. She taught us as lads in First AME Church in Gary of how to be leaders using "Robert's Rule of Order" electing officers in our missionary meetings on every Saturday, and also taught us about the Bible. She taught us how to be entrepreneurs selling popcorn and hot dogs at the basketball games in our church gymnasium. My mom's professional family, the Morris' blessed her to finish her college education at Shorter College in Little Rock, AR. Bishop S. S. Morris Sr. was the president and later became the pastor of First A.M.E.

church who built the "Morris Gymnasium where I attended church as a child until an adult.

Mrs. Jean Preston was an educator and director of the Title One Program of Gary Community Schools. She was my play mom who helped cultivate my dream in the living room of her home in Gary, along with her husband, Mr. Maurice Preston Sr., a marketing specialist who also was the first African American insurance consultant with Metropolitan Life Insurance Company in the state of Indiana.

She began with the elements of wisdom for an event and said "Darlene, you must include the 'Who, What, Where, When, and Why' in our first public meeting." My faith muscle was beginning to grow in anticipation for a demonstration of my dream product.

I remember it just like it was yesterday when God sent Erricka Coleman, an angel, who wore many hats and taught us in diverse areas to be persistent and stay on course, no matter what obstacles occurred. She branded HIAT. It took seven years, beginning in 2009 to open HIAT in 2016 when God first instructed me and told me to go and pursue in faith. I remi-nieced again on Dr. Mildred C. Harris who prophesized over twenty years ago that I would open a school. In 2009 during a prophetic service, God spoke through a prophet and said "the building and the people were already there." I fought in those two areas more than any other area in the faith process. I had never opened a public school before and I didn't know where to begin, but as I continued to seek in faith, God began to open the doors. I had some experience with Ernestine May, a teacher/principal in Gary Community School Corp. in the late 1990's when we opended a private Early Childhood School Center named Heritage Child Inc. At the time, we were both teachers. She had excellent business skills and savy which helped me tremendously. While teaching at Kennedy King, I met Ernestine, Gloria S., Gloria T., Doretha, Detrice, and Evelyn at "TABS" (Tuesday After school Bible Study) where Rita Byron was the founder which led me to Gary Educators For Christ. They blessed and asisited me with the study of the word of God in preparation for my faith journey. I also attended services at different churches where Apostle John Echkart taught in Gary, IN on deliverance and spiritual warfare which also impacted my life of faith tremendously.

My twin grandsons, Tyse and Tyres Morris, inspired me with the idea of arts and technology because they were gifted in both areas. Yes, God gave me twin grandsons—powerful men of valor is what I've call them from birth. They are both prophets. I was so happy to take care of them while their mom returned to work. I presented them in the presence of the Lord with prayer and worship music daily. I had ministry in my home, where I pastored "Dearly Beloved Ministry", where the Lord performed many miracles for His people. God was preparing me in faith for His school, HIAT, to manifest.

I was amazed to see the twins, Tyse and Tyres at the age of three working with arts and technology on the iPhone, iPad, and the iMac. This promoted the idea for HIAT to be inclusive of arts and technology. I was also a student and lover of the arts and technology.

I needed help so my wonderful associates—Mr. & Mrs. Preston Sr., Carol, Connie (deceased), Sharla, Dr. Vernetha, Denise W., Delores, Jan, Lori, Cheryl, Debra, Dr. Mary, Mrs. Alsobrooks, Minister Calvin, Dr. Conard, Rev. Dix , and sisters-in-love Brenda and Anna—assisted in the premiere planning of HIAT. Most of them became the first board for HIAT. My mother, husband, sister, and children worked in every capacity needed. Countless others helped with HIAT during this process.

I received a charter from Ball State University with great assistance from Georgette and Bob during this stage but wasn't able to open due to building and other problems which was such a great disappointment to everyone especially to the parents and over a hundred students. This was the beginning of my valley experiences. I thought my tears would never stop. It seemed as if my dream had died and my faith muscle had gone to sleep. I knew God was still there, but He seemed so far away.

My main faith partners and board members died months before HIAT hit planet Earth: my mother Dollie L. Adamson and Maurice Preston Sr., my seasoned inspirators. I believe they got to see HIAT open from heaven. My mother Dollie, the gifted teacher, from heaven was my confidant and faithfully encouraged and instructed me every step of the way. Also, after opening, I lost Connie who was my pioneer as well. My wonderful husband, Booker T. II worked in all capacities and my children: DarNieshia (Nene) was my character counselor; her husband, Terrance (Ty) was my spiritual advisor and videographer who taped HIAT's first Public Meeting at "Spill the Beans" in Merrillville with great attenders. Binika, the realtor who sought buildings for the home for HIAT, remained by my side and always had that prophetic voice of encouraging advice at the right moment. She would always send me inspiring words from Joel Osteen just at the right moment when my faith muscle was getting weak, and Joel who is always uplifting and full of joy would always strengthen me and help me to keep fighting the good fight of faith. Jamarr Booker T, my attorney in the making, legally offered his help and worked while taking law classes on line. Jasmine (Jazz) is my youngest daughter and is a quiet storm. She is the graphic designer who helped to make my visions speak in designs that made you want to shout. She is so gifted that whatever she designs today, people always ask, "Who did that?" She is presently a graphic designer for MIELLE Organics, LLC. The cover of this book was created by her.

My sister Miriam, an administrator of Specialized Services of Milwaukee Schools sent my faith muscle momentum by inviting me to visits Schools of Arts and Technology, and also invited me to attend a STEM Seminar utilizing the SMART Boards which sent a spark to ignite me. I became more inspired with ideas for HIAT.

They all worked tirelessly and never gave up with encouraging and supporting me through all of my valley experiences. There were many valley experiences in so much that I thought HIAT would never open. I cried in my bed and asked God many questions. I'm reminded: "Though the vision may tarry, wait on it, it shall surely come to pass" (Hab. 2:4). My son-in love Ty saw me crying in a vision before I experienced my season of tears. God bottles our tears in heaven. I believe that my tears were watering my prayers of faith. We must fight to keep our dreams alive! Miriam, Katrina, and Artesta all prophetesses were used throughout my faith jouney to speak prophetic utterances to keep me encouraged and on course. Dr. Nellie Williams, my professor would often call me with prophetic words to encourage me to continue to fight the good fight of faith. Gwen, Pat, Artesta, Charlotte, Mae and Denise W. were my great intercessors.

Binika, my second daughter, honored and continued with the name "Heritage" when she opened her own real estate company. She named it Heritage Real Estate, Inc. because it entails leaving an inheritance and she plans to continue the legacy. Many mornings, just at the right time, she continuously sent powerful and encouraging prayers from Joel Osteen. They were all my faith stabilizers.

My church family during the beginning of HIAT was The Love Church where overseer Apostle Rudy Gray nourished my dream with prophetic messages of patience with Vernetha, my spiritual counselor and vice; Jan, my art teacher with Marcy; Attorney Joann, my legal advisor; and Denise, my parent coordinator who worked in HIAT after it opened. Debra and Claude of "C & D Decisions" tirelessly developed HIAT's uniforms and many other HIAT promo items. Dr. Mary taped many events prior to the opening of HIAT, and even taught students how to create movies during the after school "Encore Program".

Apostle Rudy called one day and said, "Despise not the waiting room." That wasn't good news! Patience was an area I despised the most. I did despise that waiting room often. My mom, Dollie, and Mr. Preston, whom I still hear internally today, are seeing and praying for HIAT from heaven. My heart hurts when I think about how they both transitioned months before HIAT opened. They both said before they transitioned, "No matter how long it takes, keep believing."

"It will open when God says so," Mr. Preston would say often at prayer gatherings, which helped me to continue to fight the good fight of faith during this seven year journey.

I'll never forget Chris, Marla, Pam, Sharon F., Deborah, Lynn, Jan, Betty, Aida, Sharon W., Nancy, Linda and the other ladies from the Friday Morning Prayer Group in Crown Point, Indiana who tirelessly prayed with me for HIAT to manifest. Deborah Schubert was my faith partner before and after HIAT opened and continued to support me.

When pursuing a dream from God, there will always be great adversity and great opposition. The winds of adversity were blowing so strong when God was about to open His school, but God told me, "No matter what happens, keep moving forward." Mrs. Preston had prayer warriors praying with us and had prayer every Tuesday at six in the morning with the Interfaith Prayer Power Pool "IPPP", which helped to strengthen my faith muscle. IPPP prayer warriors; Rev. Vera, Rev. Marshall, Dr. Douglass, Min. Ernie, Maurice Sr., Maurice Jr., Toni, Maurice H., Rev. Shelley, Min. Marilyn, Lydia, Mary Ann, Janice, Lora (deceased), David, Mr. Williams, Joyce, Darlene and Mr. Gibson interceded and prayed.

It took intense faith as I persevered with a wonderful board. Near the end, I reflect on two faithful ladies, Dr. Jill and Linda, who were awake working with me until four o'clock many mornings seeing the dawning of many new days in my home typing and working on the proposal watching the dawning of each new day. Leona and her daughter Vinchessica worked until midnight for endless hours for grants for HIAT.

God sent Dr. Jill with such expertise to help when I was low in my valley. Dr. Jill writes books and manuals for colleges and taught me such excellence in writing and perfection in presentation of proposals and legal instruction. She practically rewrote the last proposal for HIAT.

Linda, a teacher was so faithful and even worked as a teacher in HIAT when it opened. What a blessing! These two powerful ladies had tenacity that encouraged me to continue to believe going to the sixth and seventh year of the faith journey rewriting the proposal. My faith muscle continued to grow and enhanced during this process.

My sister-in-love, Theresa, came on board and helped to enhance the technological components. Dr. Shelley assisted with the principal component as we went to IN Charter School Board during the later stages and became the first principal. The Interfaith Clergy Council interceded and prayed under the leadership of Bishop Dale Cudjoe and Dr. David Neville. Continual fervent prayer is essential in birthing your dream or product.

My granddaughter Dariyan, a great basketball player, inspired me with the athletic component of HIAT, and her mom DarNieshia was the gym teacher when HIAT opened. Pat, my play sister, and daughter Yvette offered her center, My Safari Academy, to assist HIAT with parent meetings orchestrated by Denise to help recruit students.

We went down to Indianapolis, IN time and time again trying to perfect the proposal with the Indiana Charter School Board with Michelle as the leader who was very kind and caring as she encouraged us to continue to pursue. She explained the importance of every component of the proposal being executed in perfection.

Dr. Jill said, "as many times as it takes", in faith, we will continue to be there to receive our charter from the school board." I thought to myself, *many times?* I hoped it would only take one time. I needed and had to develop patience for my faith muscle to become strong for my finished product, HIAT, to land on planet Earth. I read scriptures on patience for strength because it states: The joy of the Lord is my strength (Nehemiah 8:10). My cousin Gwen would often tell me HIAT is already open in heaven. I received joy and was often strengthened.

At last, after four times, the proposal was missing a key component, which Dr. Mia who I met at a women's prayer breakfast was strategically able to provide the missing piece as HIAT's Instructional Coach. When I was low in my faith journey and disappointed, she asked, "Do you want me to do the letter of interest?" I remember sadly saying, "I guess." My faith muscle began to intensify as I meditated on faith scriptures.

My faithful board of directors— Sharla of Work One, NW, IN Region 1 Workshop Team Lead, Sharla Sings Ministries, & HIAT's Vice President; Dr. Jill the COO of Wilbert/Pierce Colleges & HIAT's Director of Operations; Rebecca the

Attorney; Linda, the Administrator/Counselor; Minister Calvin, Chaplain of Methodist Hospital, who continued to pray and believe; Carol, Supervisor of Department of Children Services & HIAT's Secretary; Gloria, the dance genius of Indiana the dance genius of Indiana Ballet Theater; Tom, finance guru of Treehouse Financial; and George of Computer Inn Box, the technology guru—which changed over the years, went back to the state three or four times for approval until finally we got the long awaited charter approval, my long awaited manifestation. Dollie, Maurice Sr, Erricka, Denise, Claude, Debra, Dr. Mary, Cheryl, Dr. Mia, Dr. Ruthie, and Leona, my advisory board members continued to fight my faith journey with me. God always puts in place the people we need when we are processing through a journey.

In the fall of the year of 2015, after we received the charter from Indiana Charter School Board under the leadership of Michelle MeKeown and James R. Betley, we needed money or collateral. We had neither. Michelle called and stated that there is a new start up grant for charter schools. At the 23.99 hour, the Lord sent in a million dollars by faith and God's school, HIAT, is open today under Earl Phalen's tutelage,"a Phalen Leadership Academy (PLA) Network School, the Educational Management Organization (EMO). I just attended a board meeting where enrollment is over 240 students and HIAT is thriving where Sharla Johnson is the board president. The proof is in the pudding!

Prior to HIAT opening, I was attending Advancing Christ Kingdom Global Ministries (ACKGM) Apstolic Prophetic Church where my spiritual parents Apostle James and Prophetess Sharon Randolph were the overseers. They both interceded with powerful prayers and prophetic utterances. The prayer warriors of ACKGM helped birth HIAT with special care from both Deaconesses Melinda and Mary, and Oralee whom I knew previously. HIAT received great administrative assistance from members Patricia and Jacqueline. The Madkins of Airbrush Business created signs and produced gym uniforms for HIAT's students. Patricia Simes of Innovative Business Solutions also led entrepreneur business training at church, which helped me to believe the finances would appear on time. I was shaking in my boots because of the deadlines needed for the students to begin school with all of the equipment. I remember in August of 2016 watching the Fed-X semi-trucks bring in all of the school furniture and equipment for HIAT's new students. It was such a sight for my sore eyes that had cried an ocean of tears, especially during the patience process. Now, the sun was shining again.

"Fighting the good fight of faith," as Paul in the Bible stated, is so profound (1 Tim. 6:12). It was such a fight from every area, even with the school administrator of Merrillville, and it was not easy by any means. Remember my famous saying: "the proof is in the pudding." The Lord reminded me each time an obstacle appeared to keep marching forward. I reminisce on how I would lay in my bed many times asking God what happened when we didn't receive our charter. At times when I felt like giving up on my dream, God would send someone like Dr. Jill, who found me on LinkedIn, and asked if I needed any help. That was one of my lowest moments. Another low moment was when God sent Dr. Mia from a ministry who told me she would help me, and even submitted the letter of interest which had been done at least three of more times. He will supernaturally send help every step of the way to show Himself powerful. I learned that "timing" with God is different than with mankind. God may give you the vision and it may not manifest for years.

Waiting on the Lord is so important and the Bible says, "Again I say wait on the Lord" (Ps. 27:14).

It took spiritual discipline, diet, exercise, and patience. That powerful word, patience, is so key in receiving your finished product. Never stop believing and waiting on your dream to manifest. Timing is all left up to God. Our job is to keep believing and having faith in God. Don't stop exercising your faith muscle in believing that your dream or product will manifest. Discipline, diet, and routine in exercise, plus patience and faith in God will produce the long-awaited dream and product.

In June of 2016, we only had forty students registered to attend HIAT and we needed at least 150 to open. My faith muscle began to develop even more. We went from door to door, had parent meetings, advertised, made calls, visited libraries, and had many children-centered activities orchestrated by the famous Erricka with assistance from Denice Walton the parent coordinator who later was able to work as a teacher at HIAT. By the time school opened on September 6, 2016 just 2 days after my 60th birthday, I had the greatest celebration given by my family. The greatest gift was HIAT opening with 178 students registered ready to attend the first day of school. Every time I drive by HIAT and see it with my own joyful eyes, my faith muscle leaps and grows a little bit stronger. HIAT is a work in progress and I have no doubt that it will continue to soar because it is God's school.

Dr. Mildred C. Harris presented me with a leadership award for HIAT at the "Chicago Faith-Based Community Breakfast at the Chicago Hilton Hotel in 2018. She has been and continues to be such a pillar of faith throughout my life for which I am so grateful.

Heritage Real Estate Inc. is making its mark on Earth as well with my daughter Binika and my daughter DarNieshia is planning her business, All Things TyNe, Heritage Marketing + Design was opened by my daughter Jazz, and Heritage Beverage Inc. and Heritage Human Services by my son Jamarr are in the planning stages. He just incorporated Suit Shower Shave LLC. It's so important to leave a heritage or an inheritance, the Bible says. I am so happy that my college graduate children and granddaughter are working to leave a legacy on earth by having faith in God. My granddaughter Dariyan has even begun her business called The Shoe Savior. Send your shoes to Dariyan!

The Bible says having faith the size of a mustard seed can move a mountain. A mustard seed is the smallest seed on Earth. Imagine what you can do with God as the King of your life. Faith is speaking to your mountains. We all have mountains in life. As a little girl, my mom had stomach problems. I told her to tell her stomach to function as it should and it would, to both of our amazements. My measure of faith was working back then as a child. Listen to children; they have treasures within them. The Bible states "and a child shall lead them" in Isaiah 11:6.

As long as you are alive, you have faith and an opportunity to be on God's page in His plans and live according to His purpose and access His promises. Don't miss your rewards that you can receive from heaven because of your negligence of utilizing your faith muscle. He rewards them that dillengly seek him, (Hebrews 11:6). Choose to believe and have faith in God, and live eternally and blissfully upon leaving Earth in the plans God has for you. Most of all, please choose to live blissfully eternally in heaven. It will take faith in God; it's called the God kind of faith. He will supernaturally send help every step of the way.

HIAT SCHOOL PHOTO GALLERY

The Creation of HIAT School. Dreams do come true! PICTURE BY DARNIESHIA.

Dr. Darlene Henderson at HIAT School while celebrating her birthday.

Ribbon Cutting ceremony of HIAT School with the Founding Board & Guest.

Twins-Tyse, Tyres Morris & Cousin Ricco at the beginning of the dream of HIAT in 2009

Twins, Tyse & Tyres Morris, the Inspiration for HIAT School.

Niko, Tyse, Tyres, & Amanda prepare to model uniforms for a parent meeting.

The Kimani Sisters, Ms. Simmons, and Jonathan Coleman model uniforms
at the Lake County Library preparing for a parent meeting.

HIAT's "Parent Registration Meeting" for recruiting students.

The first day of school with Binika & Dr. Henderson greeting students as they arrive.

Jamarr Henderson, volunteer working on the first day of school.

Flowers sent from nephew Vernon L. Adamson III from Chesterfield, MO.

Uniforms and promotion items created by "C & D" Decisions
& portrait gift from Rev. Marshall.

Promotion items created by "C & D" Decisions at a parent meeting.

The Nicholes' boys & The Kimanis' girls prepare for the July 4 parade in Merrillville, IN.

Justin & Khari Walton & participants marching in the parade in Merrillville, IN for HIAT.

Students of HIAT School during the first year in 2016 prepare for a trip.

Music Teacher Mrs. Kimani who wrote the school song for HIAT with students.

Open House with teacher Lydia Worthington, students
& Mrs. Thelma Henderson.

Grandparent's Day at HIAT with great grandparents and grandparents of Tyse &
Tyres Morris.

Tyse & Tyres Morris' first school pictures at HIAT School

Student, Tamiah Madkins at HIAT School.

Student, Oluwapelomi at HIAT School.

Founding Board members: Dr. Mia Jones, Dr. Jill Karn, Dr. Henderson, Linda Romo, Denise Walton, & Carol King return for a visit in Nov. 2018.

Dr. Mildred C. Harris is presenting a Leadership Award to Dr. Darlene Henderson at the Chicago Faith-Based Community Breakfast at the Hilton Hotel in Chicago, IL.

My immediate family pictured left back: Binika, Jamarr, Booker T. II, Darlene, Jasmine, DarNieshia, Terrance, and Tyse & Tyres celebrating my 60th birthday two days before the opening of HIAT.

My family: Mother Dollie, Sister Miriam, Brother Vernon Jr., and extended family: Maurice & Jean Preston Sr.

HIGHER INSTITUTE OF ARTS AND TECHNOLOGY

Now Enrolling Grades K-8

HIAT School's students under the leadership of
Phalen Leadership Academies.

Granddaughter Dariyan T. Morris graduates from
University of Maryland Eastern Shores.

Dr. Henderson and family celebrate Dariyan's graduation.

7

Choose to Know Your Purpose in Life

K ing Solomon in Ecclesiastes 3:1 stated, "To everything, there is a purpose and season for everything under the sun." This includes you and me and how important it is to know our purpose in life. There is a purpose and season of blissfulness for everyone on Earth. Bliss—the shine—will occur when you connect with your creator God Almighty. Your season begins when God ordains it to begin. God will reveal your purpose to you as you develop your relationship with Him.

You should know your purpose and be adamant about blissfully fulfilling it. All you have to do is ask God. He gave us gifts and talents at birth to equip us for His good works and once you find your purpose, you will need to be determined to live it out to the fullest. Jesus, who was God clothed in the flesh, always said He was doing the will of our Father God, the one who sent Him. At age twelve, he told his parents, Mary and Joseph, that He was doing His Father's business in the temple.

God's work is business. Business brings wealth. Business began with Jesus at the age of twelve. Jesus' entire life was our perfect example of teaching us how to live a God-purpose-driven life. We were created to fulfill His purpose and His plan. Make sure your plans lines up with God's plans.

The Bible also says to make sure that we know our calling. We may have many callings and wear many hats. That may be well, but it's important to answer "yes" to the highest calling from our Creator. We all have been summoned to answer the most important call from God. It's not the pastor's job to inform you. This means that we must individually seek God and answer Him. It's the highest calling in life. We develop this by having a relationship and spending time with Him. He will reveal secrets to us. Make a sacrifice and make an appointment with God daily. He loves us so much and waits for us to spend time with Him daily.

Carry Him everywhere on purpose. He's with us every day and everywhere. Acknowledge His presence. Don't wait until it's an emergency or a life and death circumstance. Do it today and on purpose. It's the most important decision that we will ever make in our life on planet Earth.

Know that God is with you everywhere you go and He has plans and purposes for you to fulfill. Make sure you don't try to take Him into those wrong places. He may just wait outside for you.

Know this: "All things work together for the good to those who love God and are called according to His purpose" (Rom. 8:28). Everything you do should be because of your love for God. If you love God, you will obey Him. Therefore, whatever occurs in your life, be it good or bad, it will turn out for your good, because you love God and you are called according to His purpose (Rom. 8:28).

Only what we do for Christ will last. Knowing our purpose is essential for possessing eternal life. Think about it: when we all stand before God on Judgment Day, a video will play and only what we do for God will appear on your personal footage.

We all need to refocus and become God-focused for our individual purpose.

In life, we are busy doing a lot of things, but is any of it for God? Is He directing your footsteps? A wise man's footsteps are ordered by God (Ps. 37:23). You must choose to be wise with the wisdom from God.

Mike Murdock is my hero in wisdom. He is so gifted in wisdom. I'm amazed at his endless teachings on wisdom. Ask God for wisdom. When you do this, this season will change the course of your life. Man has wisdom of the world that is outside of God which will lead to destruction. It seems to be right and others will convince you that it's better than God's wisdom. The wisdom that comes from heaven is pure, then peace-loving, considerate, submissive, full of mercy and good fruit, impartial, and sincere (James 3:17). All of these will help you in fulfilling your purpose.

Earthly wisdom appeals to the senses and the emotions as we function as humans. In contrast, the wisdom that is from God reflects Him majestically and supernaturally. The role of wisdom is to know who to honor (quoted from Mike Murdock). Always honor God first, and then honor your parents. While earthly wisdom says "always follow your heart", godly wisdom tells us in Jeremiah 17:9 that the heart is deceitful above all things. While earthly wisdom says seeing is believing, godly wisdom tells us in John 20:29 that blessed are those who have not seen and yet have believed. God will make the invisible visible.

HIAT School, (the first charter school in Merrillville, Indiana), is the school I was inspired to open was invisible in heaven and became visible by the wisdom and faith in God. While earthly wisdom says "love your family and friends", godly wisdom tells us in in Matthew 5:43–47 to also love your enemies and bless them. By blessing your enemies, you will receive blessings. While earthly wisdom says "there are many ways to God", godly wisdom tells us in Acts 4:12 there is only one way to God: Jesus Christ. The contrasts assist us in choosing to discern and know our purpose for God.

We are made a little lower than the angels (Heb. 2:7) purposely, which means we have supernatural power, too. Before we get out of the bed each morning, we have to purposely make the choice to walk as a spirit versus a human (Gal. 5:16). You will be amazed with your accomplishments if you choose to walk as a spirit that possesses supernatural power purposed for eternal life.

This is the *key* to life. If you choose to walk as a spirit, you can live a purpose filled, powerful life in God. If you choose only to walk as a human in the flesh, you may live a mundane, lustful, and sinful life, full of acts like: adultery, fornication, uncleanliness, lasciviousness, idolatry, witchcraft, hatred, variance, emulations, wrath, strife, seditions, heresies, envying, murder, drunkenness, reveling, and such, which I tell you before, as I have also told you in time past, that they which do such things shall not inherit the kingdom of God nor eternal life (Gal. 5:19–21). Living this type of life without purpose will lead to eternal death.

Many of us choose to live a life without purpose and neglect to invite God into our lives. Again, this type of life will automatically entitle you to eternal death. Our purpose in life is the very meaning of our existence and without knowing this, we often suffer, ignoranance of our own significance. We fall prey to the illusion that our lives don't matter and we have no connection or impact on the world around us. The Bible is the connection that offers many insights into man's purpose on Earth and living within a meaningful mission. The mission of your purpose is all written in the Bible, which is the manual or roadmap that unfolds all of life's instructions, mysteries, and plans. It will enlighten the path of your journey beyond your dreams. God has called and elected you to fulfill your purpose. Only you can walk in your heaven-ordained shoes carefully fitted for your supernatural feet. Get busy blissfully and fulfill your purpose with God!

Conclusion

D *IBBLE* includes the requirements needed to ensure that you will spend eternity in heaven with our Lord and even your loved ones who died in the Lord. The word dibble means a tool used in boring. Boring is to force an opening or make a passage. DIBBLE is a passage to the greatest priceless gift from God given to everyone who receives Him. Remember to take heed to follow through on each of these seven choices. They are: Choice One: Choose to Acknowledge God, Choice Two: Choose to Accept God, Choice 3: Choose to Prosper and Be in Good Health, Choice 4: Choose to Be "Blessed" (Happy), Choice 5: Choose to Be Diligent in Seeking God, Choice 6: Choose to Have Faith in God, and Choice 7: Choose to Know Your Purpose in Life, Seven means completion. It's essential when it's time for you to check out from Earth that you are sure you will spend eternity blissfully in heaven with our Lord and Savior Jesus Christ. To begin this process, remember to take one moment to ask God to be Lord of your life. It is the most important decision that you will ever make in life. It will bring more joy and satisfaction than you'll ever experience on Earth. You will begin your blissful journey and you must follow the other steps and allow God to lead and guide you each and every day.

Take a nibble of my *DIBBLE* for your journey. The word "BIBLE" is embedded in *"DIBBLE"*. Within *"DIBBLE"* are many hidden bible treasures. I have given you seven simple steps to ensure that you make it to heaven blissfully upon leaving Earth. Jesus is coming back soon and you must complete these seven steps to ensure you are heaven-bound. Once you leave Earth, it's not the end, but the beginning of where you will spend eternity.

You'll never be the same and life will be filled with blessings beyond your dreams. As Bishop T. D. Jakes—a powerful bishop whom I love and have learned so much from, and I have followed during my journey—would say, "Get ready, get ready, get ready!"

DIBBLE: Do It Blissfully Before Leaving Earth!

Love Nuggets

G od is love! We must all walk in love to enter the kingdom of God to possess eternal life. When you accept Him as your personal Savior, the love process will begin. It's extraordinary and supernatural.

Love is the most powerful element that we should sprinkle upon our lives and others. It brings us into our purpose and calling of loving God, ourselves, and others. Love God because He loved us first. It's a forever love affair.

He will bless you beyond your imagination and He won't let you figure Him out. When you think He's coming from the north, He will come from the south. If you think He's coming from the east, He will come from the west. He keeps you in expectation and excitement. He will bless your socks off and keep you in a wonderful, blissful and glorious life here on Earth. You will begin this love affair as a babe in His glory where He will carry you upon His wings of the eagle, carefully gliding you through your life experiences little by little.

Second, you must choose to love yourself. Believe it or not, many of us don't love ourselves. It begins in the womb, if your mother or father rejected you. It progresses in life in your inner man, especially if you were rejected as a child and heard negative things about you from key people in your life. Rejection is a horrible spirit that will follow you everywhere you go in life. If you reject yourself, you most certainly won't love yourself. This will open the door for others to reject you which will lead to making bad choices. Simply making bad choices is proof that you don't love yourself.

None of us are perfect. We all make mistakes. To err is human. The only man who never made a mistake is Jesus, who was our perfect example. Forgive yourself and others quickly. Don't think about it. Just say it and your actions will follow. It's not about our feelings.

Remember: continually making bad choices means you possess self-hatred. This is why you must choose to love God and yourself. Next, think before speaking because life and death is in the power of the tongue, that little unruly member between your teeth. Studying to be quiet is essential because then you can listen more with both of your ears, internally and externally.

Since life and death is in what we speak, everything we speak in life should be seasoned with salt. Just enough salt will do. Too much salt will destroy your food and no salt will taste blah, especially in our choices as we speak. It is the same in life. Some things in your life, you need to speak to with just enough salt, and some things you need to speak death to without any salt, which means you don't need to say it. We can be trapped by our own words. Lastly, just enough salt gives such a delightful taste and a good word with just enough salt spoken in season is golden.

Since life and death is in the power of our tongues simply means we should speak life and when something is over, let it die. Learning this will bring a life of good fruit. Learning whether something should continue or it shouldn't is key.

Now that you love yourself with your tongue, you can love your neighbor. Do it simultaneously like the Bible says: "love your neighbor as you love yourself." It's easy this way. You wouldn't do anything intentionally to harm yourself, so you won't intentionally do anything to harm your neighbor.

Now, you will go through the "glory" process where you will learn how to walk as a spirit, experiencing all of the unpleasant events in life because it rains on the just and the unjust, which means unpleasant events will occur to all of us. How you handle these experiences will determine if you will become better or bitter. A lot of people become bitter instead of better through life's trials. We all have these fiery trials, as our Heavenly Father calls them.

It's essential that you persevere through these glory experiences because the sun will surely shine again. You must pass the test. After passing the countless tests, you will return to the divine glory. We always win. It's all in your perception. It's the final state of living blissfully on Earth before leaving Earth! It's a state of mind and it will happen.

Love is the power that will turn your world upside down into a state of blissfulness. The world will know we are Christians (Christ-like) by the love we show. It's easy to love someone when they love you in return. To love someone when they are unlovable is being Christ-like, God-focused, and God-purposed. Life will continue to give us lemons in life. When it happens, add sugar by deciding to be the sugar in life. Now add that sugar to the lemons, and you will have lemonade. I love lemonade and you will too. Perseverance is the process that translates you to the state of blissfulness. This is the blissful experience. I hope you enjoyed a nibble of my *DIBBLE*.

New Found Love

I've looked all of my life
For a love which would suffice,
All of inner longings
Would be satisfied just belonging
TO
This awesome New Found Love
Sent all the way from Heaven above!
It is so exciting and vivacious.
It is so contagious and bodacious,
BECAUSE
This New Found Love that I have found,
Is all I need to abound,
To reach the heavenly shore above,
Jesus, Jesus my New Found Love!
NOW
Jesus, My New Found Love,
All I'll been waiting for.
Jesus, My New Found Love
Your name radiates from heaven above!

By Dr. Darlene A. Henderson

Jesus Is Coming Back Soon!

Jesus is coming back just like He said He would!
Don't get distracted and do as you should
He's coming back just like a thief in the night
Get your bags packed and make sure you're right!

It's getting later than it's ever been before.
The earth is really shaking oh more and more!
Nature is preparing for Jesus it's so amazing!
But the world is busy partying and even hazing!

Jesus said in His word He had to shorten the time.
If he didn't even the saints would be left behind!
The trumpet will sound as he appears in the sky!
As the world continues to get drunk and high.

Satan is tricking almost everyone!
Deceiving with his tricks and even his guns.
Jesus has already prepared his daughters & sons
Please pay attention to His precious little ones.

Jesus is coming back just like He said He would!
Don't get distracted and do as you should.
He's coming back just like a thief in the night.
Only if you're ready will you make the flight!

By Dr. Darlene A.Henderson